The Sis Chronicle

English Language
The Sis Chronicle
(Anthology Of Children's Literature)
Compiled by
Sharjah Indian School Boys, Juwaiza

Published in November 2024
by Decan Imprint Publishing Co.
Reg. Off: Sharjah Publishing City
Free Zone Sharjah, UAE.
Phone: 00971-561127998
Email : decanimprint@gmail.com

Cover Painting : Harliz Biju Varghese

Cover Design : Prasanth Mangad

AED 16
21/24-25/Sl.No.21/50/NS 15.4
ISBN 978-93-5973-807-9

The Sis Chronicle

Compiled by

Sharjah Indian School
Juwaiza

DECANIMPRINT

About the School

Sharjah Indian School is owned and managed by Indian Association Sharjah. Gaining the long span of experience from the main school of Sharjah Indian School at Ghubaiba (Estd 1979), we have started functioning at Juwaiza, on 19th February 2019 with the name SHARJAH INDIAN SCHOOL, BRANCH JUWAIZA. The school is affiliated to the Central Board of Secondary Education (CBSE) New Delhi (India).

The large demand of a school with a moderate fee structure to cater the needs of the Indian Community in the UAE has been the key aspect to think in the direction of starting a new school. Our school accommodates boys of grades I to XII. All amenities required for the student life are getting organized in the school. The great expertise of our teaching faculty is the biggest asset of our school. Our campus is made with the commitment to nurture the nature around us by planting more trees and plants.

Our school is an eco-friendly campus which holds vegetable gardens and the other plantations.

We focus on academic excellence, mutual respect, self-discipline, faith in challenges, and community service to achieve personal goals now and for the future. We are committed in providing quality education to the Indian Community living in the UAE.

We encourage the enlightening process in all relevant areas, leadership and active learning, and encourage critical thinking and technological skills to realize our full potential.

We hold faculty and students alike to the high standards of

intellectual and moral development. Hence empowering them to become successful and efficient personalities to excel in their chosen fields. We will focus on external factors that enable improvements to facilities and new building projects.

The aim of the school is to impart education, laying stress on the intellectual, physical, mental, social, aesthetic and moral development of the children.

The school thus aims at making its own contribution towards establishing principles of social justice, equality of opportunity, genuine freedom, respect for religious and moral values enshrined in the constitution of India in conformity with the social standard of living and etiquette existing in U.A.E.

The school has drawn out a comprehensive educational system to bring out the latent talents and abilities of the children. Various co-curricular and extra-curricular activities are provided to develop the total personality, team spirit and leadership qualities to face challenges in life.

Through teaching and example, faculty members strive to guide their students to a personal acceptance of faith and to a respect for the life-long educational process.

Shajrah Indian School is committed to the cultivation of individual potential and to the graduation of sincere, educated and articulate citizens.

FOREWORD

Dear Readers,

It is with immense pride and enthusiasm that we present the latest edition of *The SIS Chronicle*, a true reflection of the vibrant spirit, creativity, and talent of the students at Sharjah Indian School, Juwaiza. This magazine is not just a collection of articles—it is a celebration of the thoughts, dreams, and achievements of our student body.

Within these pages, you will find a wide array of contributions that showcase the diverse perspectives of our school community. From imaginative short stories to inspirational poetry, each piece reflects the passion and dedication of our young writers and artists. Our contributors have explored various themes, creating a platform for dialogue and reflection.

This magazine is a testament to the power of expression and the importance of nurturing creativity in every student. We are incredibly proud of their efforts.

We invite you to delve into these pages—to enjoy, reflect, and be inspired by the voices of tomorrow. On behalf of the entire team, we thank you for your support and hope you enjoy this journey through the thoughts and talents of Sharjah Indian School, Juwaiza.

With every good wish,

Mohammed Ameen
Principal
Sharjah Indian School, Juwaiza

Content

The Intriguing Obsession

MUHAMMED ADAM

5 C

It was a cold and breezy day. My friends, Waiz and Sai, decided to join me for football at the nearby ground. As we arrived, I noticed a pigeon, ready to take off, flapping its wings towards the next building. I'd always been obsessed with the idea of flying like Superman.

My friends took up a challenge, "C'mon, bro! Let's try flying!" I replied, "Are you crazy, bro? That only happens in movies or dreams!"

Still, Sai and Waiz tried to flap their arms, but alas, they just stood on the ground, unmoved. It was my turn. I flapped my arms with all my might, and lo and behold! To my surprise, I was flying!

"What magic is this?" I uttered to myself in awe. My friends gasped, watching me in wonder. The higher I flew, the more superheroic I felt.

Soon, I could see the whole of Sharjah—the giant wheel of Qasba, the Flag Island, and the blue waters of Majaz. Everything looked beautiful from up here. I kept flying and soon reached Dubai. I saw the Museum of the Future, the Dubai Frame, and even reached the topmost floor of the Burj Khalifa. I was super excited to reach the top without

any entry fee!

Then, I decided to fly to Paris and see the Eiffel Tower, which had been my dream for a long time. I knew it was somewhere towards the West, soaring up through the Black Sea. I thought, "Why not try my luck and save my dad the cost of a ticket to Paris?" But I started feeling tired and wanted to land somewhere. I reached the revolving restaurant in Abu Dhabi and thought of eating something, but then remembered that I was broke.

So, I took a rest under an apple tree, ate some apples, and then took off again towards the West. I flew and flew until I reached a desert with trees but no water. I was exhausted, thirsty, and completely lost. I started praying to God to save me. I was missing my family and my friends, all because of my greed. I started sobbing badly.Suddenly, I felt the earth shaking. I woke up to my mother asking, "Adam, are you okay, my child? You must have been dreaming something bad!" Of course, it was just a dream. Hurray! I hugged my mom and said, "Thank you for waking me." She looked puzzled.

I learned a lesson that day: I will never again become obsessed with fiction, and I will focus on real life and real people, not superheroes. I got ready for school, excited to share my intriguing experience with my friends. I will never forget this dream—though unrealistic, it was fun to think about.

School Days
MADHVESHA SRINATH
4A

Once there was a boy named Marco who lived in Sharjah, U.A.E. He was 8 years old and studied in Grade 3. His school's name was Sharjah Indian School. Today was his first day of school, and he was very happy. He made new friends, and the best part of his day was when he was selected as the class monitor (the student who looks after the class when the teacher is not there).

When the teacher gave him work, he did it smartly. However, one day, Marco was not paying attention in mathematics class, so the teacher asked him a question. The question was: **$100 + 100 - 90 \times 100 + 10 = ?$**

Marco quickly calculated the answer and said, "The answer is 120."

The teacher confirmed that he was correct, and everyone was surprised.

A few days later, the Term 1 exams were around the corner. When the exam results were announced, the teacher said, "Children, Marco and Arjun have both scored 100 out of 100 in the Term 1 exams, so I will be making Marco the *Star of the Month* and Arjun the *Student of the Month* for June." Everyone clapped for them.

Then, it was time for summer vacation.

Never Give Up on Your Dreams
AARON VARUSH
5D

One day, in a village in India, there was a small boy named Rahul. He wanted to become a space scientist. He played with toy rockets and spaceships, watched videos about space, and read various books on the subject. As he grew older, he studied how to build a spaceship, fix broken spacecraft, and ensure a soft landing. He worked harder and harder with each passing day.

Eventually, he landed the perfect job as an aerospace scientist at ISRO. He began constructing his first spacecraft. After three years of hard work, he named it Victory 1 and sent it to the moon. However, as it was about to land, one of the rockets failed, and it fell roughly into one of the craters.

Rahul was devastated and stopped working for months. But then he remembered his mother's words: "Never give up on your dreams." Inspired, he returned to work on Victory 2. When it was ready, he sent it to the moon in search of the remains of Victory 1.

When Victory 2 landed, its AI greeted the AI of Victory 1 with a cheerful, "Hey buddy!" Everyone was surprised and overjoyed, and they celebrated the success of Victory 2.

Whose Diamond?
ABDUL HADI
7 I

Once there were two friends named Patrick and Liam. Liam was rich, and Patrick was poor. One day, while Patrick was walking through a forest, he saw something sparkling. Curious, he went to check it out. To his amazement, he found a diamond. Speechless, he took the diamond home.

A few days later, while talking to Liam, Patrick mentioned the diamond.

"Liam, while I was walking through the forest, I found a diamond," Patrick said.

Liam, intrigued, asked, "Where did you keep it?"

Patrick, trusting Liam, replied, "I kept it on the shelf in my house."

That night, all Liam could think about was the diamond. Jealous of Patrick's fortune, Liam quietly went to Patrick's house and stole the diamond. The next morning, when Patrick couldn't find his diamond, he went outside and saw a large crowd. When he approached, he realized that Liam was showing off *his* diamond.

Patrick shouted, "Give me back my diamond!" But no one believed him. How could a poor man like Patrick have a diamond? Frustrated, Patrick decided to seek help from the king.

Patrick explained his story to the king, who ordered his men to find Liam. When Liam arrived, the king asked, "Liam, how did you get the diamond?"

Liam confidently replied, "I bought it from the jeweler."

The king then commanded his men to bring the jeweler.

Soon, the jeweler arrived. At first, the jeweler said Liam was innocent. Patrick began to panic, fearing that he would lose his diamond and be punished. But the king warned the jeweler, "If we investigate and discover that Patrick is innocent, you will not escape punishment."

Frightened, the jeweler confessed, "Liam promised to pay me a large sum of money if I said he was innocent."

Upon hearing this, Patrick was relieved. The king declared, "This proves that Patrick is indeed the owner of the diamond. As for Liam, his punishment is to give half of his wealth to Patrick."

Patrick was overjoyed at the outcome.

The Giant Red Spot
ARYAN BINESH
5Q

Everything went well until one of the astronauts, named Oliver, disappeared. The other team members, while wandering through space, came across a tornado where a screaming figure caught their attention. As they moved closer, they realized that the howling creature was Oliver. They rushed to rescue him, but unfortunately, they encountered another tornado.

Fearing for their lives, they ran as fast as they could. After what felt like an eternity, the tornadoes finally disappeared. Relieved, they were happy to have found Oliver safe. They walked for a while, searching for a way out.

Suddenly, they felt the ground rumbling, but they assumed it was just Bob's stomach, as he was hungry. Bob then asked, "Why are you all looking at me?" Just then, they all turned around and screamed, "Ruuuuuuuun!"

But Jessica suddenly stopped. She heard radio sounds coming from their speakers—it was the International Space Station! The station informed them that their backpacks had return ropes. Quickly, they pulled out their return ropes and safely reached the space station. From there, they took a spacecraft and returned to headquarters.

Back on Earth, they reunited with their families and lived peacefully.

The Haunting of the Well
ASTIN JIHN NINAN
4E

Once upon a time, there was a well where some children loved to play. One day, a girl named Jenni fell into the well and tragically died. Her parents were heartbroken, and after her death, they decided to move to another city.

Soon after, a man named Smith bought their old house. One night, while he was sleeping, he had a nightmare about the well. In his dream, he saw a girl emerging from it. He was watching it on TV and thought it wasn't scary at all. But suddenly, the girl started coming out of the TV. She was holding a knife and running toward him, intent on harming him.

In his dream, she stabbed him, and he felt the pain as he died. Suddenly, he woke up to find a knife exactly where she had stabbed him in his dream. Shocked and terrified, he realized that he had indeed been harmed.

From that day on, no one dared to enter that house ever again.

The Lost Purse
MUHAMMAD ZAYED
5E

Once there lived a boy named Andrew. He was playing in the park when suddenly he tripped on something. He looked and found a purse with lots of money inside it. Andrew was so happy. He had always begged his dad to buy him a new bicycle, but he also remembered what he had learned in school about honesty. Andrew looked in the purse and saw an address card. He went to the house and returned the purse to its owner. They thanked Andrew for his honesty and rewarded him with a bicycle.

The Kind Waiter
MUNZIR ABDUL NAZAR
6M

Once upon a time, there was a waiter at a restaurant who was kind-hearted and loyal to people. One day, he saw two homeless individuals in the street asking for food and money. The waiter gave them some food and money, making them very happy. They thanked him profusely, and the waiter felt good about what he had done.

The next day, he saw the two homeless people fighting with his restaurant owner. When he asked what had happened, the owner replied, "Poor people shouldn't come to my restaurant; only the rich people are welcome."

The waiter said, "They have money to buy food."

The owner responded, "I don't want poor people coming from the street; I only want wealthy customers from luxurious places."

When the homeless people heard this, they sadly left the restaurant. The waiter felt bad for them. The owner then warned him, "If you help them, I will fire you from your job."

The waiter was disheartened by this. The next day, he saw the two homeless people begging again in the street. The owner called the waiter to throw away some excess food that was fresh but had been prepared the day before. The waiter said, "This food is fresh; why should we throw it away?"

The owner replied, "If our customers want good food, we have to prepare it fresh because our customers are rich."

The waiter responded, "Then why don't we give this food to the poor people on the street?"

The owner retorted, "If you give it to the poor, I will fire you from this job."

Feeling sad, the waiter went outside to throw the food in the garbage. However, he saw the two homeless people asking, "Please, can you give us this food?" The waiter decided to give it to them. When people in the street saw

this, they began clapping and cheering for the waiter. A boy recorded the scene on his mobile phone live.

Hearing the commotion, the owner came outside to see what was happening. He called the waiter over and informed him that he was fired. The waiter felt extremely sad.

The next day, while the owner was taking care of customers, people from a live TV channel entered the restaurant and said, "We saw you helping people on the street in a viral video."

After seeing the video, people started flocking to the restaurant and buying food, which made the owner very happy. This time, the two homeless individuals came to the restaurant. The live TV channel asked them, "Did this owner help you?"

The poor people explained everything that had happened and mentioned the waiter who had helped them. When the waiter arrived at the restaurant, the homeless individuals pointed at him, saying, "He is the one who helped us."

The TV crew asked the waiter, "Did you work here?" He explained that he had been fired for helping the poor people and spoke about the owner's greedy behavior.

The customers felt upset and left the restaurant. The owner, now feeling sad, watched as the restaurant was closed by the authorities due to public outcry. A new restaurant was opened for the waiter as a reward for his good deeds.

The Monkey and the Rat

OM JHA

5 N

Once upon a time, there lived a monkey who ruled the forest. One day, after eating his meal, the monkey fell asleep under a tree. A little rat was also playing nearby. The little rat began running up and down on him, which soon woke the monkey. The monkey caught the rat in his hand and said, "You little rat, how dare you wake me? I will kill you!" The rat got frightened and requested the monkey, "Pardon, O king,

please do not kill me. I am a little creature. Please let me go; I will help you in the future." The monkey laughed and said, "You are too small to help me. Anyway, you can go."

A few days later, the monkey was playing in the jungle when he found himself caught in a hunter's net. The monkey screeched loudly, but he failed to get free. He pleaded, "Help me! Help me!" The rat, whose life was saved by the monkey, heard the screech and ran to him. "Don't worry, my friend. I will save you," the rat said.

The rat gathered all his friends and told them, "We all have to help my friend and set him free." The rat and his friends cut the net and set the monkey free. The monkey was saved and thanked the rat, and from that day on, they became the best of friends.

The Story of a Kindful King
TIMOTHY THACHARAYIL SONY
6H

Once upon a time, there was a magical kingdom in France. There was a faithful king named James. He had a loving mother, and her name was Elizabeth. One day, a thought came to the king's mind to expand the kingdom for a little more land. So, the king gave everything like food, water, clothes, and other supplies to the soldiers.

But one day, the commander of the soldiers went to the king and spoke, "Oh, Majesty, we have bad news to tell you. The things that you gave to us have been stolen." The king was astonished; he jumped out from his throne and said, "What! The things that I gave you are stolen? I command you to go and find the thief right now and beat him with belts in the middle of the people!" The soldiers gave a good salute and went to find the thief.

After two hours, they caught him, covered him with a black blanket, and went to the king's office. When they reached there, the king was waiting for them. The commander said, "Oh, Majesty, we have both good and bad news." The king said, "Please tell me the good news." The commander replied, "The good news is that we have successfully caught the thief in the capital city. And the bad news is that the thief is none other than your favorite and loving mother,

Elizabeth."

The king was surprised but sad to hear that his mother was the thief. However, a command is a command. So, he took the hands of his mother and went into the middle of the people. He took off his royal dress and put it on his mother. Everyone was confused, and the king said to the soldiers, "Forgive my mother and beat me with belts."

Everyone was crying with sadness and understood the relationship between the two people.

So the moral of the story is to love others, for love is a precious and joyful feeling that should be handled with the utmost care and etiquette. With a proper sense of morality, one can find happiness in their relationships and not be overcome by lust, cherishing their loved ones for who they are instead of what they have.

Cursed Creek: Death's Eerie Echo

CHRIS BINAY BIJU NAYAGAM
10F

In a small, secluded town nestled in the heart of the forest, three friends—Peter, John, and Thomas—often sought adventure to escape their mundane lives. On a misty Saturday morning, they decided to explore the outskirts of the town near a murky creek, fueled by curiosity and a longing for something extraordinary.

As they ventured deeper into the woods, the atmosphere grew increasingly eerie. Twisted tree branches reached out like skeletal fingers, and a heavy silence enveloped them. The creek's water flowed sluggishly, reflecting the gray clouds overhead. Unease gnawed at Thomas, but his friends' excitement was contagious, so he followed along.

The trio's laughter echoed as they skipped stones across the water, momentarily forgetting their surroundings. That's when they noticed a figure stumbling towards them, a man hunched over and limping, his skin a sickly shade of gray. Thomas felt his heart race as the man drew closer, his labored breathing audible.

"Hey, are you alright?" Peter called out, concern lacing his voice.

The infected man's head jerked up, revealing bloodshot

eyes and a mouth twisted into a smile that almost looked like a snarl. Before they could react, he lunged at them with inhuman speed. Instinct kicked in, and they scrambled back, John pulling out a pocketknife while Peter grabbed a sturdy branch.

"Stay back!" John yelled, brandishing the knife shakily.

The infected man let out a harsh, otherworldly growl. As he approached, they saw something horrifying—pulsating blue veins like ropes that seemed to writhe beneath his translucent skin. The forest seemed to close in around them, the air thick with a tinge of fear and terror.

Thomas's fear transformed into determination to survive. He reached into his backpack and pulled out a small device he had been tinkering with—a gadget meant to emit high-frequency sound waves designed to kill any pathogen, an experiment in sound-based defense mechanisms.

Without a second thought, he activated the device. A high-pitched resonance filled the air, and the infected man staggered, clutching his head as he emitted a scream of pain. The sound waves seemed to agitate the virus within him, causing visible tremors.

Seeing an opportunity, John lunged forward and plunged the pocketknife into the man's side. The infected man let out a final, throat-ripping cry before collapsing to the ground, his body convulsing before finally going still.

Breathing heavily, the three friends exchanged a mixture of relief and shock. The forest felt less oppressive, as if the very atmosphere had held its breath during the encounter.

"What... what was that thing?" Peter panted, his knuckles white around the branch he still held.

Thomas looked at the lifeless body, his mind racing with thoughts. "I think... I think it was some sort of experiment gone wrong. A virus, maybe engineered in a lab. That device I used... it disrupted its cellular structure. We need to report this to the authorities."

As they left the creek and made their way back to town, the weight of what they had encountered settled upon them. Their friendship had been tested in ways they could never have imagined, and the shadows of that day would forever cast a different light on their adventures.

But tragedy struck again when night fell. As the moon hung low in the sky, a chilling wail echoed through the forest. A horde of infected creatures emerged, their eyes gleaming with an unnatural hunger. The friends fought valiantly, their weapons slashing and striking against the advancing nightmare. But in the midst of the brutal battle, John was overtaken by the sheer numbers. He fell to the ground, his screams piercing the night, as the creatures tore him apart.

Heartbroken and terrified, Peter and Thomas managed to fend off the creatures, watching as they retreated back into the depths of the forest. The loss of their friend was a wound that would never fully heal.

The survivors stumbled back to town, haunted by the horrors they had witnessed. The memory of John's sacrifice and the brutality of the battle would forever linger in their minds, a constant reminder of the thin line between life and death, and the depths of darkness that could be unleashed by human curiosity.

The Homeless Man
and The Dog
ELVIN BIJU VARGHESE
5F

Once upon a time, there was a homeless man who was begging on the street for money. One day, a dog came to the homeless man for food, and the homeless man gave his last food to the dog. The dog ate it, and this repeated for several days until they became friends. One day, animal control came by the street. The homeless man did not want to give up his dog. When animal control came to take the dog, the homeless man begged them to give his dog back, but they didn't stay long enough to hear his words. The dog was put up for adoption after several days.

A rich family came to adopt a dog from the animal shelter. They bought a dog, and it was the homeless man's friend. The dog went to his new family. After a year passed, the family went for a walk outside and took the dog with them. Suddenly, the dog noticed a familiar face—it was his old friend. The dog ran to him, and the homeless man was so happy. The dog's new owner was confused, but the owner's daughter said they should take the homeless man to their house.

The father told her, "We cannot take the homeless man to our house because he is a stranger." She replied, "My teacher told me we should help people in need." Feeling sorry, the father agreed, and they took the homeless man to their house. The homeless man saw the inside of a home for the first time in his life. He lived with the dog forever.

The Story of Chuckleburg

ADEEP GOPI
6G

Timmy and Andy, two mischievous kids, discovered the power of laughter in their quiet town of Chuckleburg. Through their playful antics and hilarious pranks, they transformed the town into a hub of joy and laughter, drawing in residents and visitors alike. Chuckleburg quickly became known for its sense of humor, and the town embraced its identity as the happiest place on earth.

As the years went by, the legacy of Chuckleburg continued to grow. A beautiful legacy garden was established in honor of the Chucklebug Chronicles. Statues of Timmy, Andy, and the Chucklebug stood tall, surrounded by colorful flowers and engraved stones that carried laughter-inducing quotes.

Timmy and Andy combined two of their biggest hits, organizing a Chuckleburg Carnival Cruise. The ship featured amusement park rides, carnival games, and comedy shows, creating an unforgettable floating festival of fun. Due to popular demand, a second and third Carnival Cruise were launched, offering even more laughter-themed entertainment.

The residents of Chuckleburg gathered together for the grand Legacy Gala, celebrating the enduring impact of the town's unique culture. Timmy, Andy, and the townspeople shared stories and laughter-filled memories, reflecting on the journey that had shaped their lives and connected them through humor.

The town stood as a beacon of laughter and unity. Timmy, Andy, and generations of residents gathered in Chuckle Square. The Chuckleburg glowed in vibrant neon, and a monumental chuckle storm formed in the sky, releasing confetti that showered the town with colorful mirth. The legacy of Chuckleburg lived on, reminding everyone that laughter was not just a mission, but a way of life.

Nature

AARON SHIJU
10K

In nature's arms, a world so grand,
Where life and beauty go hand in hand,
The forests are tall, the oceans wide,
In nature's embrace, we find our guide.

The gentle rustle of leaves in the breeze,
Whispering secrets among the trees,
A symphony of birds in morning's light,
Nature's chorus, a pure delight.

Mountains reaching for the sky,
With snow-capped peaks, majestic and high,
Rivers winding, carving their way,
Through valleys where wildlife frolic and play.

The sun's warm kiss upon the land,
Painting landscapes with golden hand,
And when the night descends so deep,
The stars above their vigil keep.

Beneath the waves, a world unknown,
A vibrant, underwater kingdom shown,
Coral reefs in color so bold,
A treasure trove of stories untold.

From vast deserts to green meadows,
Nature's wonders can't be unseen,
In every corner, beauty resides,
A tapestry of life, where love abides.

So let us cherish and protect this Earth,
The place that's given our lives their birth,
For in nature's embrace, we find our worth,
A precious gem, this planet of great mirth.

Fish

ABHINAV RAJ
4L

I am a fish,
With colors so bright,
I breathe through my gills,
In waters so light.
I glide with my fins,
Through rivers and seas,
In the water, I'm free,
At home with the breeze.
But if you catch me,
I won't survive,
Out of the water,
I cannot thrive.

Dreams, dreams

ANTONY JOHN
11E

My dream is my genie
because dreams make
my dreams come true.
Where the eyes
see the light though they
thought they'll only see the dark.
And the body feels
something or somewhere
that was far from their reach.
From thinking and thinking
can help you experience even if
it is pricy
it is far far away
it is time-consuming.
A dream is a ticket
to anything you want.
Even if you know
you won't really get it.

The Clock
ANTONY JOHN
11E

Although the clock
Relocates its hands,
From time to time,
It is always busy
But still gets time to smile
At 10:10 AM and
At 10:10 PM,
After that minute,
It goes back to tedious ticking.

Love Your Reflection

We have to hug the mirror
In order to see our true beauty.

Taps Hold Tears Too

At times, I'd see the tap dripping tears,
I turn its handles, its dripping clears.

At the Double Door

At the double door,
If one door won't budge,
Go through the other.

"Be Water, My Friend"
JESHWANT RAJASEKHAR
9H

'Be water, my friend, so fluid and free,
Change and adapt, like the boundless sea.
Strong and precious, a blessing and curse,
The source of life's refreshing verse.
One tiny drop, harmless and kind,
But together, they can create chaos combined.
Disastrous yet vital, lessons we learn,
In water's depths, we discover hidden strengths.
"Be like water," Bruce Lee once shared,
Flow with grace; no challenge should be scared.
Embrace flexibility, with spirit unbound,
In simplicity's beauty, greatness is found.

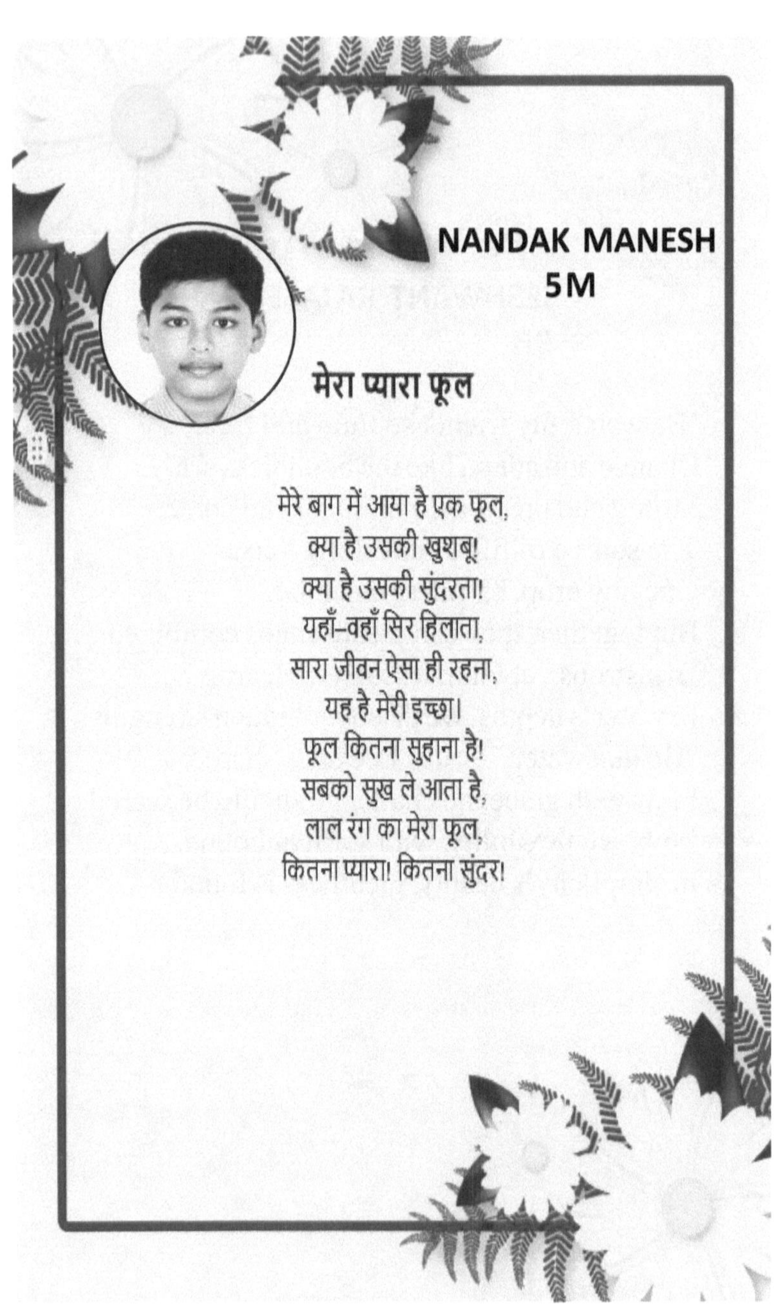

मेरा प्यारा फूल

मेरे बाग में आया है एक फूल,
क्या है उसकी खुशबू!
क्या है उसकी सुंदरता!
यहाँ–वहाँ सिर हिलाता,
सारा जीवन ऐसा ही रहना,
यह है मेरी इच्छा।
फूल कितना सुहाना है!
सबको सुख ले आता है,
लाल रंग का मेरा फूल,
कितना प्यारा! कितना सुंदर!

A Trip to Moon

PRANAV SURESH

5M

"Let's go to the moon,"
my mother said.
"What shall we take?"
"Butter and bread,
add some of this
and some of that,
and please do take the
fly-killing bat!"
We packed our bags
for the next day,
but Oho! The rocket left yesterday.

Magical Beasts

SAIFAN SAMEER

4P

Decades ago, a world filled with beasts,
So long and short, so tall and small,
Some with amazing power and some bland.
There are predators and prey,
It's a fight-to-the-death,
A fight for food or die trying.
Some eat flesh, some eat plants,
And some eat both,
With some thirsty for blood
And stomachs rumbling for food.
Others have food right next to them

But are being hunted.
It is the survival of the fittest,
But some of the tiniest ones
Can lead to your death.
No matter how strong you are,
With just some teamwork,
You can crumble like paper.

The Parrot

SIDHARTH GANESH
4L

The day when I met a parrot,
It was green as a leaf,
The beak was red as a cherry,
It can imitate a human.
It hops-hops and hoops-hoops,
With its friends and family happily.
It went back to its place,
And what a wonderful day it was.

Little Brother

AFZAAN AHAMMED

2S

I was eight,
and all I could
do was wait
for the day you come—
oh! you little plum.
You look so pretty,
like a kitty.
You make me happy,
you little naughty.
You are so fun
and my loving son.

Memories

MOHAMMED ZAYAN O P
6I

My memories of the past
elegant and beautiful.
My sadness is in the past,
and happiness in the future.
Oh, I see brightness rising in my future,
rumble and thunder in the past.
I love my past and future,
emerging future from my dreams,
sadness setting like the sun.

Passion in My Heart
AHAMED NAEEM ANSHAR
9G

I have a passion in my heart,
Waiting for the right moment to start.
But I know that the moment is now,
For I shall get there someday, somehow.
I have a dream in my heart,
Getting ready to adopt the art,
Shining like a star through the streets,
Figuring out mysteries and ditching the cheats.
This is a work unfit for the weak,
For there is no rest throughout the week.
Fighting for justice for this, just may
Be the light for the ones who pray.

I have a passion in my heart,

Waiting for the right moment to start.

But I know that the moment is now,

For I shall get there someday, somehow.

The Journey of Life

SABIQ MOHAMED

12A

"Life is a precious gift from God,"
my mother says.
Be happy and enjoy all the days.
For some, life is great,
But others see life with hate.
It is complex, filled with problems,
stress, and distraction.
For some, it is blessings, happiness,
laughter, and attraction.
We all are passengers in the journey of life,
Where we come across a lot of strife.
We all have different paths along the way.
We learn a lot here, but we're never meant to stay.
Our destination is farther away and
greater than we know.
For some, the journeys are quicker,
and for others, it is slow.
So better busy ourselves with doing good deeds,
Which are useful for the life after death we need.
When the journey finally ends,
we'll receive a great reward:

Find everlasting peace, together with our Lord.
"Life is a precious gift from God,"
my mother says.
On life and life after death,
I can write long essays.

Racism
RISHIKESHAV SUNILDAS
6N

I know you will never buy
a black ramen,
Always buying golden
Oreos and things.
Think you're an American,
but you're European.
The time you got a black dog,
 you painted it like a
white.
When you got black pants,
you threw them in
the trash.
Racism is not good for our future;
Respect everyone, because
we are always one.

Racism is nothing in this world.

The future is in our hands!

We got shaped,

and we should shape the future.

Hard Tears

RAHUL PALANI

10K

Tears of pain tell a story;
Tears of joy tell a story.
No matter how it is, a tear—
Crying is a stress buster,
No matter in joy or in stress.
Tears are endless,
never mind what others say;
It's your right to cry or to die.
But just look behind and smile;
Your disparities will shine bright.

That's My Teacher
MIRTHICK ABHINAV RAGHAVAN
6H

Like the sun,
You always shine.
Like a flower,
Your smile always blossoms.
Like a friend,
You always stand with me.
Like a mother and a father,
You always care for me.
Like a magician,
Your teachings become magical.
That's why
You are my favourite teacher!

A Voyage to
The Endless Ocean

ADITHYA ELAVAZHAGAN

12C

Life is just like the ocean.
Just like how life counts every minute,
An ocean is complete by every water droplet in it.
Every good moment will come
and go with a bliss,
Just like how the sea waves
and ends with a kiss.
Adventuring it is like voyaging
the edge of a knife,
Finding the destination is a one-time
opportunity in life.
Life will swing memories that rock to and fro,
How every wave meets each other with a flow.
Even the ocean has a dark side
where shadows prevail,
But there was once a point from
which something as
bright as life used to hail.
So don't be sad if things don't turn out well,

Because the stars in the sea at night will
show a way and tell.And now your voyage is ending
near the end of the world-
Would you let your destiny face the wall,
or would you let it uncurl?
This twirl of fate will be yours to swirl.

Sky
**GAUTHAM GANESH
11E**

Oh! My Beauty,
Oh! My Sky,
Show me your beauty!
You look happy when
You are blue,
You look sad when
You are hidden.
Don't let the clouds
Hide your fairness,
Don't let their jealousy
Take off your aura

That makes you invisible.
Break the barriers
That clouds have set for you,
Break the doors of darkness
That confine you from the universe,
Elegant enough to be left undiscovered.

Nature

**MOHAMMED DANISH KHAN
5C**

Nature is lovely,
Nature is funny.
Nature is nature—
Save it for the future,
Or face the consequences;
It will be out of our senses.

Care about nature—

It's the care about the future.

Nature is nature;

Make it safer.